The Facts on Famous Artifacts

PRESERVING THE U.S. FLAG

Dwayne Hicks

CREATED BY Humans

Published in 2027 by The Rosen Publishing Group, Inc.
2544 Clinton Street, Buffalo, NY 14224

First Edition

Editor: Greg Roza
Designer: Michael Flynn

Photo Credits: Cover Carmen K. Sisson/Shutterstock.com; (series background) Yuliya Chsherbakova/Shutterstock.com; (flags) pp. 4, 6, 14 upstock/Shutterstock.com; p. 5 Zack Frank/Shutterstock.com; p. 7 https://commons.wikimedia.org/wiki/File:Betsy_Ross_1777_cph.3g09905.jpg; p. 9 f11photo/Shutterstock.com; p. 11 https://commons.wikimedia.org/wiki/File:Placing_the_Stars.jpg; p. 12 Jon Bilous/Shutterstock.com; p. 13 Everett Collection/Shutterstock.com; p. 15 https://commons.wikimedia.org/wiki/File:Fort_McHenry_flag.jpg; p. 16 https://commons.wikimedia.org/wiki/File:Original_Star_Spangled_Banner_on_display.png; p. 17 https://commons.wikimedia.org/wiki/File:Repair_Work_on_Star-Spangled_Banner.jpg; p. 19 (top) YES Market Media/Shutterstock.com; p. 19 (bottom) Lukasz Szwaj/Shutterstock.com; p. 20 https://commons.wikimedia.org/wiki/File:US_33_Star_Fort_Sumter_Flag.svg; p. 21 https://commons.wikimedia.org/wiki/File:Fort_Sumter_storm_flag_1861.jpg; p. 23 (main) Bradley Molnar/Shutterstock.com; p. 23 (inset) https://commons.wikimedia.org/wiki/File:Phoenix-Arizona_State_Capital-1901-US_Arizona_Flag.JPG; p. 25 (top left) https://en.wikipedia.org/wiki/File:First_Iwo_Jima_Flag_Raising.jpg; p. 25 (top right) https://en.wikipedia.org/wiki/File:Raising_the_Flag_on_Iwo_Jima,_larger_-_edit1.jpg; p. 25 (bottom left) https://commons.wikimedia.org/wiki/File:IwoJimaFlag.jpg; p. 26 kasman vector/Shutterstock.com; p. 27 https://en.wikipedia.org/wiki/File:Ground_Zero_Spirit.jpg.

Cataloging-in-Publication Data

Names: Hicks, Dwayne.
Title: Preserving the U.S. Flag / Dwayne Hicks.
Description: Buffalo, New York : Created by Humans, an imprint of Rosen Publishing, 2027. | Series: The facts on famous artifacts | Includes glossary and index.
Identifiers: ISBN 9781534553255 (pbk.) | ISBN 9781534553262 (library bound) | ISBN 9781534553279 (ebook)
Subjects: LCSH:Flags--United States--Juvenile literature. | Emblems, National--United States--Juvenile literature.
Classification: LCC CR113.H53 2027 | DDC 929.920973--dc23

Manufactured in the United States of America

Some of the images in this book illustrate individuals who are models. The depictions do not imply actual situations or events.

CPSIA Compliance Information: Batch #CSCBH27. For Further Information contact Rosen Publishing at 1-800-237-9932.

CONTENTS

STARS AND STRIPES

The Stars and Stripes has long been an important symbol in American culture. It's a very common sight in the Unites States, hanging proudly in front of homes, government buildings, and businesses across the country. The U.S. flag has appeared in many different **versions** over the years. Each new state means a new star on the blue field, so the design has changed over time.

Many flags from U.S. history can be found behind glass in museums around the country. Many are tattered and falling apart. Why should we work to preserve these artifacts? Let's learn about several important U.S. flags to find the answer.

One of the earliest versions of the American flag is known as the Fort Stanwix Flag.

"Resolved"

On June 14, 1777, leaders in colonial America made the following announcement: "Resolved: That the flag of the United States be thirteen stripes alternate red and white, that the Union be thirteen stars in a blue field representing a new constellation." Some historians believe it was first flown over Fort Stanwix, now in New York State. Today, we celebrate Flag Day on June 14 each year.

THE BETSY ROSS FLAG

Perhaps the most well-known story about the U.S. flag is that the first official flag was created by seamstress Betsy Ross during the American Revolutionary War (1775–1783). This is a story that has been told to American school children for a long time. But is the story real?

In 1776, Betsy Ross was a seamstress in Philadelphia. Popular stories say that George Washington himself visited Ross in June of 1776 to ask if she would make a flag for the new country. Ross reportedly made suggestions about the design, including changing the six-pointed stars to five-pointed stars.

In this painting from 1920, Betsy Ross is demonstrating how easy it is to create a five-pointed star out of fabric.

Despite the long history of celebrating Ross as the creator of the first stars-and-stripes design, historians have determined that most of the story is just that—a story. The first person to reveal the story was Ross's grandson William Canby. In 1870, Canby wrote an article titled "The History of the Flag of the United States." Canby stated that his article was based on family stories and his own **recollections**.

Although Ross most likely did not create the original Stars and Stripes, we do know that she was a Philadelphia seamstress who created flags and banners for the U.S. Navy.

ARTI-FACT!

Ross ran an **upholstery** shop in Philadelphia for many years with the help of her daughters, granddaughters, and nieces. They made many U.S. flags. Ross finally retired at the age of 76. She passed away on January 30, 1836, at the age of 84.

The Betsy Ross House in Philadelphia is reportedly where Ross first created the Stars and Stripes. Today it is a museum.

THE STAR-SPANGLED BANNER

In the summer of 1813, during the **War of 1812** (1812–1815), Major George Armistead was commander of Fort McHenry in Baltimore, Maryland. He learned the British would soon attack the fort. Armistead hired Mary Young Pickersgill to make two U.S. flags. One was a "storm flag," a durable flag to be flown in bad weather. The other was a huge "**garrison flag**" that measured 30 by 40 feet (9.1 by 12.2 m).

ARTI-FACT!

Each of the stars on the garrison flag measures 2 feet (61 cm) across. Pickersgill used cotton for the stars, which was not very easy to get in those days.

This painting, made in 1962 by Robert McGill Mackall, shows Pickersgill and her nieces sewing the garrison flag while Armistead and other U.S. officers watch over them.

Armistead wanted to make sure the British saw the U.S. flag flying over Fort McHenry as they approached. This is the flag that became known as the Star-Spangled Banner.

In September 1814, U.S. lawyer Francis Scott Key boarded one of many British ships waiting in Chesapeake Bay. He convinced British officials to release his friend Dr. William Beanes, who had been arrested. The British made them wait in the boat Key arrived in because they were about to attack Fort McHenry.

Key and Beanes watched the battle from eight miles (12.9 km) away. The **bombardment** lasted 25 hours. Key and Beane waited all night for it to end. When they saw the garrison flag still flying the next day they knew the British had lost the battle.

Fort McHenry

When "dawn's early light" broke, Key saw that the garrison "flag was still there." Key wrote these famous lines on the back of a letter while he watched the Battle of Baltimore. He titled this poem "Defense of Fort M'Henry."

Armistead kept possession of the garrison flag. When he died, his wife Louisa took possession. She was probably the person who sewed an upside down V on the flag. She may have been sewing a letter A for Armistead. Historians believe Louisa was also the person who first starting giving away pieces of the flag.

When Louisa died in 1861, her daughter Georgiana Armistead Appleton inherited the flag. She loaned it to flag historian George Preble in 1873. He briefly put it on display in Boston, Massachusetts. Appleton allowed Preble to give away more cuttings of the flag. That practice continued until the 1880s.

Preble first had
the garrison flag
photographed in 1873 in
the Boston Navy Yard.

When Georgina Appleton died in 1878, her son Eben Appleton inherited the flag. He loaned it to the city of Baltimore for a celebration in 1880. The flag remained in a vault until 1907, when Appleton loaned it to the Smithsonian Institution in Washington, D.C. In 1912, Appleton officially gave the flag to the Smithsonian for permanent display.

The Star-Spangled Banner was in tatters. The Smithsonian hired embroidery teacher Amelia Fowler to lead efforts to restore the flag. Fowler's team of seamstresses removed the canvas backing that had been added in 1873. They spent eight weeks adding a linen backing.

The Star-Spangled Banner has gone through several rounds of repair since Fowler's work on it. Today, the Star-Spangled Banner is displayed in the National Museum of American History (NMAH) where it is protected from further damage.

Missing Pieces

The Armistead family gave away over 200 square feet (18.6 sq m) of the flag to veterans of the Battle of Baltimore and other people of importance. Some of these cuttings have been recovered and are on display in the NMAH or other museums. Some cuttings are in private collections. The fifteenth star has never been recovered. There are several rumors about its whereabouts (could it be buried with President Abraham Lincoln?), but none have been confirmed.

OUR NATIONAL ANTHEM

Key's famous poem, inspired by the attack on Fort McHenry, appeared in the *Baltimore Patriot* newspaper. Soon after it appeared in newspapers across the country with the title "The Star-Spangled Banner." The poem was often sung to an English tune from the 1770s titled "The Anacreontic Song." This version of Key's poem became the U.S. national **anthem** in 1931.

ARTI-FACT!

"The Anacreontic Song" was the official song of the Anacreontic Society, a gentleman's group of **amateur** musicians in London, England. The original version is a celebration of the ancient Greek poet Anacreon, who wrote lyrical poems about love, celebrations, wine, and other mature themes.

Key's original poem was much longer. "The Star-Spangled Banner" is just the first stanza, or part, of the poem.

The Star-Spangled Banner

O say can you see, by the dawn's early light,
What so proudly we hailed at the twilight's last gleaming,
Whose broad stripes and bright stars through the **perilous** fight,
O'er the **ramparts** we watched were so **gallantly** streaming?
And the rockets' red glare, the bombs bursting in air,
Gave proof through the night that our flag was still there.
O say does that Star-Spangled Banner yet wave
O'er the land of the free and the home of the brave?

THE 33-STAR FLAG

On December 20, 1860, South Carolina announced that they were seceding from, or leaving, the United States. This was one of the major events before the American Civil War (1861–1865). In response, U.S. Major Robert Anderson moved U.S. soldiers into Fort Sumter in Charleston Harbor, South Carolina.

Anderson had a 33-star garrison flag raised over the fort. It was 20 feet (6.1 m) by 36 feet (11 m). For three months, the giant flag showed that the United States would not recognize any talk of secession. Once the war started, the flag was replaced by a smaller storm flag.

Today, both the garrison flag and the storm flag are held by the National Park Service. Experts are discussing how to preserve them. Shown here is the storm flag that flew above Fort Sumter during the battle.

Return of the Flag

After Anderson's forces were defeated at Fort Sumter, he took the garrison flag to New York City, where it was displayed on a statue of George Washington. In 1865, after the Northern states won the Civil War, Anderson returned to South Carolina and raised the historic flag once again over Fort Sumter. The garrison flag and storm flag were once on display at the Fort Sumter National Monument, but they are now in protective care due to their age.

THE USS *ARIZONA*

On December 7, 1941, Japan attacked the U.S. naval base in Pearl Harbor, Hawaii. More than 350 Japanese planes used bullets, bombs, and **torpedoes** to destroy U.S. warships and planes. The USS *Arizona* battleship exploded and sank. Around 1,177 crewmembers died, and around 900 are still **entombed** in the sunken *Arizona*. This was the event that pulled the United States in to World War II (1939–1945).

In the days after the attack, U.S. servicemen found a flag that had been on a boat on *Arizona*'s deck. That oil-stained flag is on display at the Arizona State Capitol Museum.

ARTI-FACT!

In 1958, U.S. Congress approved the construction of the USS *Arizona* National Monument. However, not enough funds were available for the project. In March 1961, rock star Elvis Presley held a concert to raise money for the memorial.

Today, you can visit a memorial built over the sunken wreck of the *Arizona*. The U.S. flag is flown 24 hours a day over the site.

THE FLAGS OF IWO JIMA

Iwo Jima, an island in the South Pacific, was the site of a major battle between the U.S. Marine Corps and the Imperial Japanese Army during World War II. U.S. forces wanted to take control of the island because its location would help them in the war. The United States won the battle after 36 bloody days.

To celebrate the victory, U.S. Marines set up an American flag atop Mount Suribachi. However, Marine Corps officials wanted a larger, more noticeable flag placed there. Five Marines and one photographer returned to Mount Suribachi to place the new flag. This is one of the most iconic American photographs ever taken.

first flag

second flag

The flags raised at Iwo Jima had 48 stars. Hawaii and Alaska did not become official states until 1959. Today, both of the Iwo Jima flags are on display in the National Museum of the Marine Corps in Triangle, Virginia.

ICONIC IMAGERY

The American flag has appeared in many memorable photographs. The photograph of Marines placing the flag on Iwo Jima, taken by Joe Rosenthal, won a **Pulitzer Prize**. It has become a lasting symbol of American strength in war.

Can you think of any other famous flag photos? You may think of the American flag placed on the moon in 1969 by U.S. astronauts Neil Armstrong and Buzz Aldrin. You may recall firefighters unfurling the Stars and Stripes in New York City after the 9/11 **terrorist** attacks of 2001. These iconic images of the American flag show the lengths to which Americans will go to protect and honor their country.

What does the American flag mean to you?

Photographic Artifacts?

Photographs can be considered artifacts when they document human history. Joe Rosenthal's prizewinning photograph of Iwo Jima captures a moment (well, the second moment) of U.S. victory over the country that bombed Pearl Harbor. It carries a lot of meaning for Americans and represents a **pivotal** moment in history. Photographs are also physical objects much like other artifacts, such as flags, documents, pottery, tools, and more.

PRESERVING THE PAST

Why is it important to preserve artifacts like the Fort Sumter flags and the flags from Iwo Jima? Artifacts can tell us a lot about the events and people to which they are connected. Preserving artifacts helps us to preserve our rich history.

Just standing in front of the Star-Spangled Banner in the NMAH helps one imagine what Francis Scott Key saw when the sun came up and the garrison flag was still flying over Fort McHenry. It helps one understand the human effort needed to create such a giant flag and then preserve it over the years. It makes you think about the people who have interacted with the artifact throughout history.

TIMELINE

1776	Stories say George Washington asked Betsy Ross to make the first American flag.
June 14, 1777	The Second Continental Congress announces the first official design for an American flag.
1813	U.S. Major George Armistead hires Mary Pickersgill to make two U.S. flags that will fly over Fort McHenry.
September 1814	The Battle of Baltimore is fought; Francis Scott Key pens "In Defense of Fort M'Henry."
April 12–13, 1861	The Battle of Fort Sumter and beginning of the American Civil War
1865	The 33-star flag is raised over Fort Sumter once again after northern forces win the American Civil War.
1870	William Canby writes "The History of the Flag of the United States."
1931	"The Star-Spangled Banner" becomes the national anthem of the United States.
December 7, 1941	Japanese forces attack Pearl Harbor, sinking the USS *Arizona* and other ships.
February 19–March 26, 1945	The Battle of Iwo Jima
August 12, 1959	Hawaii becomes the fiftieth U.S. state and the American flag is updated to the version we know today.

GLOSSARY

amateur: One who does something for fun, not as as job.
anthem: A song of praise or gladness.
bombardment: A sustained attack with artillery, or bombs.
entombed: In a final resting place, as in a tomb.
gallantly: In a spirited and heroic manner.
garrison flag: The largest flag flown in the United States, most often for national holidays and other special occasions.
perilous: Including a risk of being injured, destroyed, or lost.
pivotal: An extremely important time or moment.
Pulitzer Prize: Any of various annual prizes, including outstanding literary or journalistic achievements, established by the will of politician and newspaper publisher Joseph Pulitzer.
rampart: A protective wall or barrier.
recollection: Something from the past that is remembered.
terrorist: Having to do with the use of violence to achieve political goals.
torpedo: A bomb fired underwater that is shaped like a tube.
upholstery: Having to do with materials used to make soft coverings for furniture.
version: A form of something that is different in some way from forms that came before it.
War of 1812: A war fought in North America between the United States and Great Britian mainly over trade policies and the British imprisonment of American sailors.

FOR MORE INFORMATION

BOOKS

Lusted, Marcia Amidon. *The Star-Spangled Banner: Introducing Primary Sources.* Mankato, MN: Pebble, 2020.

Zee, Amy Van, and Melissa Crawford. *The War of 1812: Independence Secured.* Ann Arbor, MI: Cherry Lake Publishing, 2026.

WEBSITES

American Flag
www.usa.gov/flag
Learn more about the American flag and other U.S. national symbols.

National Museum of American History
americanhistory.si.edu
Check out the many historic artifacts housed at the NMAH, including the Star-Spangled Banner that flew over Fort McHenry.

INDEX